STRING QUARTET or STRING ORCHESTRA

Leroy Anderson for Strings

Arranged by
William Zinn

EL 03451

Cover photos: Peter Perri, Warren Rothschild

The Typewriter

Violin I

Leroy Anderson
Arranged by William Zinn

EL03451

Sandpaper Ballet

Leroy Anderson
Arranged by William Zinn

Forgotten Dreams

Leroy Anderson
Arranged by William Zinn

A Trumpeter's Lullaby

Leroy Anderson
Arranged by William Zinn

The Waltzing Cat

Leroy Anderson
Arranged by William Zinn

Copyright © 1950 MILLS MUSIC, INC. (Renewed)
International Copyright Secured   Made In U.S.A.   All Rights Reserved

The Syncopated Clock

Leroy Anderson
Arranged by William Zinn

Sleigh Ride

Leroy Anderson
Arranged by William Zinn

13

EL03451

Belle of the Ball

Leroy Anderson
Arranged by William Zinn

Plink, Plank, Plunk

Leroy Anderson
Arranged by William Zinn

* Tap music with bow

EL03451

Blue Tango

Leroy Anderson
Arranged by William Zinn

Jazz Pizzicato

Leroy Anderson
Arranged by William Zinn

Horse and Buggy

Leroy Anderson
Arranged by William Zinn

Copyright © 1951 MILLS MUSIC, INC. (Renewed)
International Copyright Secured   Made In U.S.A.   All Rights Reserved

Serenata

Leroy Anderson
Arranged by William Zinn

EL03451

Jazz Legato

Leroy Anderson
Arranged by William Zinn

EL03451

Fiddle-Faddle

Leroy Anderson
Arranged by William Zinn

The *String Builder* Series

by Samuel Applebaum

Samuel Applebaum's STRING BUILDER series is the string class method of the BELWIN COURSE FOR STRINGS. The STRING BUILDER series is designed to have the Violin, Viola, Cello and Bass play and learn together throughout. Each instrumental book, however, can be used separately for class or individual instruction on that particular instrument.

- realistically graded material
- musical interest combined with technical value
- a world-wide best-seller in string education

Versatile and comprehensive, the STRING BUILDER series provides the quality string instruction for which the late, great educator Samuel Applebaum is famous.

String Builder, Book I
- ____ (EL 01542) Teacher's Manual
- ____ (EL 01543) Piano Acc.
- ____ (EL 01544) Violin
- ____ (EL 01545) Viola
- ____ (EL 01546) Cello
- ____ (EL 01547) Bass

String Builder, Book II
- ____ (EL 01548) Teacher's Manual
- ____ (EL 01549) Piano Acc.
- ____ (EL 01550) Violin
- ____ (EL 01551) Viola
- ____ (EL 01552) Cello
- ____ (EL 01553) Bass

String Builder, Book III
- ____ (EL 01554) Teacher's Manual
- ____ (EL 01555) Piano Acc.
- ____ (EL 01556) Violin
- ____ (EL 01557) Viola
- ____ (EL 01558) Cello
- ____ (EL 01559) Bass

3rd and 5th Position String Builder
- ____ (EL 01935) Teacher's Manual
- ____ (EL 01936) Piano Acc.
- ____ (EL 01937) Violin
- ____ (EL 01938) Viola
- ____ (EL 01939) Cello
- ____ (EL 01940) Bass

2nd and 4th Position String Builder
- ____ (EL 01941) Teacher's Manual
- ____ (EL 01942) Piano Acc.
- ____ (EL 01943) Violin
- ____ (EL 01944) Viola
- ____ (EL 01945) Cello
- ____ (EL 01946) Bass

University String Builder
- ____ (EL 02137) Teacher's Manual
- ____ (EL 02138) Piano Acc.
- ____ (EL 02139) Violin
- ____ (EL 02140) Viola
- ____ (EL 02141) Cello
- ____ (EL 02142) Bass

Belwin's Best-Selling Music...

for String Orchestra

VIVA VIVALDI
arranged by Owen Goldsmith
____ (BSO 00057)

AFTERNOON WALTZ
by Owen Goldsmith
____ (BSO 00062)

SLEIGH RIDE
by Leroy Anderson
arranged by Samuel Applebaum
____ (BSO 00020)

THE OLD CAROUSEL
by Owen Goldsmith
____ (BSO 00061)

SONATA IN F (The Glorious)
by Henry Purcell
arranged by Robert Klotman
____ (BSO 00059)

for Orchestra

DANCE OF THE SUGAR PLUM FAIRY and WALTZ OF THE FLOWERS
by Peter Ilyich Tschaikowsky
arranged by Merle Isaac
____ (CO 00154)

MARCH OF THE NUTCRACKER and TREPAK
by Peter Ilyich Tschaikowsky
arranged by Merle Isaac
____ (CO 00155)

MARRIAGE OF FIGARO (Overture)
by Wolfgang Amadeus Mozart
arranged by Merle Isaac
____ (CO 00163)

NEW WORLD SYMPHONY (First Movement)
by Antonin Dvorak
arranged by Merle Isaac
____ (CO 00164)